Strange Days

Pull the tides to your side,
swim along & dream on;

Rhea

CONTENTS

In case of Fire

Shivla Shikwana

Silver moon ready to
liberate the shadows
swinging on the loose
frail ends of our cathartic
drug from what will always
be yearned

Walk through any
door & unlock
the stars.
Take one step closer
toward a new pulse.
Normal to run,
but normal has gotten
you nowhere
but sleep

Pupils dilated,
screaming toes form
the mellow mind.
Take a look in the
mirror, witness the pure
pure form of your ideas
trapped from within your body

Young girl
soft latitudes
bridge of love
sacred nights
filled w/hollow harmony
carousals set to the melody
of wolf like cries
lingering to the
call of the hour

My hair so dark like aged wine
drink the years away
old & fine
I love to see the holy & kind
the blood & water
the cork & screw
Teach me to split the wood grain
and plant the seeds
to be sweet born bitter
loved by some or sipped by all

the farmers gift
to be sweet born bitter

Does the swamp grow w/every flood
or is it networked within?
Are the alligators blind or worse, confused?
How quickly did you learn the
directions to distractions?

Shared alleyways walked
on separate nights
Mirrored reflections
of midnight luminescence
bouncing from brick to brick
A story repeated for
those who follow that
same friendly alleyway

Smug in the hum
of American land
nights dawn soaked
our moon has a plan
tell the people
our moon has a plan
sheer madness will soon starve
innocent madness
(a world spins)
deserts & beaches share the grain
accompanied by creatures that play
hollow chains dividing the lane
clustered by the active youth
letting them know what cloud
rained the hardest
never telling why
It's rude to call mother's
Miracles in nature's circle
we were wise enough to step outside
even wiser to give names to phases
educating natures four as one divinity
Religion is missing a fourth
the children worship in God & not
nature, universe & awareness

Hey solider can you give me your gun
it's time to cook the chief's choice
I want to eat before my last death
& drink the old Whisky from the
underground cellar
I am not a war
Soon red borders fill the page &
everything sane will spoil to
stupid lunacy
Colors will wed & live
under a domicile state

A great rift for cowboys & Indians
sharing their horses & elderly to the river
folding The Nile to gold filigree
let's find a new tomb
one built with the ashes
of a spring born hill
dipped & saturated in
fervor of new calm

Sweet bright gloom
help me to lose sight
as I sit thru this nite
I want to follow my words
and take the venom away
& sell it to medicine men
medicine to cure the blind
we've come a long way to
not see the fangs on the head

Why do we exist?

-we are only here to learn how to die
-teaching us how to become it
-not learning when to become it

She's a lost
Lonely world
Sent out to the sea
She steers the ship
To an unknown dream
Paralyzed
By her fear
Of being stuck
To a broken ship

Present as a wave
She whispers into the fray
Silver trees reflecting her prey
Unspoken, unwoven
Her ethos pure as emotion
She's distracted by the day
Before the avalanche
Causes rain
Now she waits
For a stormy drain
To overflow the
Dam before the valley
She stays

Corrupt child in the Spring of March
skyline heights possible silver washed
out of sight as the whole evolution
begins to take leap into an opulent river

Virtuous sinner
repurposed to bring on the joy
let's climb to the top & get a little higher
it's happening right now
seamlessly unattached & unaware
giant pools of dead snakes
around the corner as it waits
Existing as a demonstration
a spark to light the fuse
an execution for the fool

I am trapped w/the cool
complacent land of our tailing spine
in which we drive on
A flow towards tranquility
causing the common soul to
stay behind
Feel the bridge with your barefoot
dangerous steps neighboring the veins of your
dripping blood
changing the dirt to new acuity
Causing the earth
to erupt instantly
The symbols of your name set to elaborate
twirls and spins & promoting a call
breaking all the plates in the attic
cutting to obedience as trained
interesting to see what is &
what was that made you turn
could've been me but I'm losing my grasp
insanity & drunken wolves are the only things pure
bitter wine & fallen apples are what remain good
reside into the plum of the pit
desired to sail
asking for a portrait to be made
by the unknown artists w/new lines that
refined the culture to stand with his ear

(Intermission) Intermission

Voices in my head have found us
goddess of Adonis & love
in green rich tonic
tantric aura blinding grown men
who owns my words
where does my mind
get its thoughts from
Vigilant scholars apostatized
by futile wealth
come outside where the Sun is red
getting tired of your gentle lawn
w/its stream filled flowers
& bushes of fertilized death
is it night yet?
all lawns look the same at night
all homes look the same inside
movements of naturalistic rhythm
boiling to unearthly steeples
wise ossuaries surrounded w/ancient secrets
immersed in new discovery
a burden to universal time
Will you still consider the cosmos
it's freedom baby, free to be numb

Friendly women in artistic ecstasy
exercising the new rules of mystic dynasty
dining on the families of impecunious appliqué
adapting to the benevolent children
                              of fledge-forth flight
fighting the curse of tomorrows witch
wondering what hex will be swiftly given
garnished in howling cacaesthesia
corrupted? Not yet
yenning for unsettled settlements
shroud of terror
                              trapped in casting beauty
                              bonding the outlaws
organizing the symphony to an undeveloped route
ruling the years into fabricated permanence
patrolled by a joint parlance of arbitrary negligence
narrating our trusted belief in ubiety
utilizing effervescent visualizations
vindicating the white walls of cool xanadu
                              (xat constructed zen)
zipping the parted sheets into a matching quilt
questioning the troubled hero
hindered to her futtock mirth
masking the infected cognizance of beloved joy
jeweled in deliberate intuition of limitations
learning to kindle our woven incepted kitchen
keeping the spoiled monster to a cratered image

Subtle beat to race the panic
new to the steps of rhythm
                    old rhythm
swept in a remedy of guitar & soul

A L I V E

walk down her arms
in summer chills
proof that fire exists
felt w/out the heat
an endless paradise
tied to the 2nd sun

_____

**Even the smallest things
can hold a chaotic shadow
to the most ordered lights;
paper with no lines**

A monster of pulsating structure is requested
for the village to torch the entire premise
While we age in agony
run w/science & conquer the objections
gifts of the ghetto
sculpted & prepared
Murder is written in the program
forest of measure
the girl roams free from promise &
is irrational in the confessions of rationality
to identify as a choice strong will of fluid dwellers
paranoia is real when all else fails
help is on the wrong face
Status gap
a jump in the curve
no part in content as the
concern of spectators are audiences
in the dynamism of an actor
rather to be stationed in repent
pleasure is worn
in fantastic mystery
presiding as seeds for the fruits we bear

She within certainty provides value
like the reflection upon a mirror lake
waiting & watching
her curvature
her spine
the salutary greed cycles in her free-command
her entrance to the waking world
placing the presence of an unknown
in the center that she holds

-The red alarm is used in moments of emergencies

and she plays the music as her own
a motel room near highway
unnoticed to the cars & cracks of the road

the voice she controls is worth the weight
her choice for revival in the coming hours
linger in the days that followed
ensuring her love was reborn

Death will great you, death will meet you
take your things, take your time
we are not souls of the path we've taken
I can hear the sounds of the shrunken tides
burnt ember mist
a wandering man in a lonely isle
not in Colorado anymore
or beside the midnight sleep

The medicine man who asks for more
or the solider who asks for more
to get the people softer
to move our seconds faster
get out alive
get before the eyes
nothing is ours, take it all

Gold sodden month
or grasshopper
inching toward the cavities of our ancestors
I've let this go on, far too long

Cars seemingly drive on mass burial grounds,
paved by the natives during times of quiet
affairs. Let me see your luggage & the things
you've brought w/you for this trip. Furnished
ivory in the house of plenty. Poachers arrive
with one skill, a total democracy. They promise
serenity but offer acceptance, as if you had a
choice. You fell in their trap & locked eyes with
the man across the mirror. There is no safety net.
Before & after have meant the same thing since
the first killing was displayed. A transfer of
revelations kept unknown. People in their right
state of mind have become critical to weird
showings of scars & souvenirs

Sweat dripping from the forehead,
glowing on hot ebullient beaches
in presence of human confrontation.
Imminent peril seas cast out over pieces
of wrecked servility. Do it again, do it
once more, & this time don't look so
surprised when it grabs ahold of you.
The canals are built to gently carry a
certain amount of gold, without the
use of machines on both ends for
both travelers. Give validation, & watch
how an image already developed, distort
along the edges. Our only solution is
to burn the evidence without adversity.

Glaciers gliding through
the gaps of the ocean
they construct a
circle on a sphere
the musical has just begun
watch the ice tango
into slabs of white
take the green flash from
the sun & cast it to the folded
cracks of a transparent wave
from the shaking hands that
shatter the snowflake upon
the touch of its frost

King cobra transcribed in Latin scripture
still alive as he makes his way
to suffocate his prey
a 1000 year old skin
live crypts
nursery songs
angels w/white lustrous
costumes & glowing Coriolis
emerge in desire
kneel to stand
fissuring as the bread expands
until it greets another
until our minds can read each other's

Wisdom for the ageless
but I know a truth
and when one truth is unraveled
all lies are naked

The King Cobra needs no arms
the water needs no taste

mankind is behind

Remember
remember remember
light the rooftops
take over the schools
sneak off in the middle of it all
so that no one can find your home
we got the music
we got our secret
right here
as part of
some system

I'm not an animal
I'm not stuck behind
in some broken dream
of a hesitant child
left to gather
left to cores
his waking mind

Some will say it was for a chance to be recognized
or it's because they didn't have a say in the matter
however it's told, we still got a lot of work to do
they're a lot of decedents right in front of us
who want you to believe as they do
think & do as they do
but if no one is functioning
in their realm of free-will
then there's no one to rule &
any hierarchy begins to fall apart
causing a circular paradox to take shape
we have been tricked in recognizing this
as the only system in place to offer habitation

A real long time ago, between the first kids gaining
fresh new wisdom as agents of growth
and being forced to sell their innocence
for cognitive comprehension
stood a juncture of etherous influence
that went missing when
settlements epitomized residents

Doing what our lovers told us
turning on our bedroom light
casted in the shadows hide
putting everything
and all
to the hum
that made us fall
it's going to hurt when
we hit the ground
but not as bad as when
we were birthed.
We were volunteered to
know the air
chocking on
our nerves

Back in those days we were fragile uncut opalescence
Honey furnished the hive masking our progress
a halt of horror was established as the pearl shroud
created conceivable penchants that never met totality
Expired & malt
gorilla paws in depths of vines just as
Milk moved the tides. Long & wide
we have stumbled inside the touch of celebration
A trail faded in preclusion
what benign culture sculpted traditionally
fractured the unfettered expansion
Buy the ticket &
nuance of smooth yellow rays
contribute to our definitions
lose your pride
lose your purpose
tryst where our lives first began
where we met on that hill above it all
Bask the placid fruit
undeveloped & moot
like Spy's of the luxuriant mosaic lizard
tokens of latitude invoke on channeled strips
showing me the forbidden stream
the lumberyard in full swing and
dower wastelands taunted the malevolent bindings
beside the point that's fixed in rage
placing haggard roses on a theater stage

There is a place down south
so far down it has no latitude
the locals are without way & have lost all contact
satellites orbiting Earth can touch all axes
they can recall the chords we play as their own
sell it, use it, or toss it
in antecedent structure
coiled metal
a target is on my back
modalities

        huntsman
        search among the sieges
        off to work

and I thought you came from the coliseum
hips to sway & shape the form of our rotten clay
untouchable sounds
uncouth from my premise
ensure your gatherings
as one fortune reading would tell you
to settle your debts & clear your threats

Hey there, you need anything?
Exotic cats, fresh fruits, the stem of an
atrosanguineus?

I shouldn't tell you this but
the cosmos is out to get you
and we're all watching, waiting, for you to do
something, or someone.
You're on your own, like always.
But there is something you should know that
the women & men won't want to know.

What happens after you regain consciousness?

I came here yesterday ready to leave
my saddlebag is empty and buried beside me
This is essential to life, everything but life
While the rest of us are cooking a show
you will be there, in Egypt with one voice.

Do you remember when we left the city?
The snow was everywhere & I could see
your breath from the car.
We drove through the night, trying to escape
The snow occupied everything
from the Hotel Rm.

We drank the punch like it was our own

**Slopes curve with infinite
passion, nature has one rule:
to define Earth**

Shivla Shikwana

What's going inside the neighborhoods
in the suburbs & cul-de-sacs?
There's something strange happening
all the homeowners are part of a collective hive
still photographs being acted out as religious callings
but inside murder has ensued
slaughters served for breakfast

"Use the knife Jimmy, and don't spill it.
We don't want another mess on our hands"

nobody has cleaned up since last Tuesday
the doors are left open & pushes everything on a path
windows draped over, leaving the feet to never dry
then mail arrives & people step out in absence
causing the brain to misfire our nerves
paranoid devoid of fate results because of this
confusion is our next answer; our first is nothing
but by the time we reach our resolution
we're back inside, to do it all over again

This world is afraid of the places we can go
Anywhere all the time
And we gave it all up for a person to declare
What is fair or certain in each of our lives
But if you never stepped out from the city of lies
Then everything will remain so wrong & pass by
That's how our future will end

We could change it all
One night to break the wall
Leave the mind alone
How'd we end up in here
In front of this stone
We're lost in our game
Until we meet again
That's how our future will end
That's how our future will end

Never looking back into our past
Left w/only a moment to spare
That's how our future will end
That's how our future will end

I
am charmed
spellbound
by
the
creation
of words
it is beyond
universe
clattered
hills
can change
a river
to navigate land
send
the message
I am
never
coming
home

Professional professors
professing professionally,
providing proper persistence
proficiently. Preparing
pondering preluding premium
prudent positivity,
perpetrated perfectly.
Predicting preliminary
products proposing progress.

Great Orphan Child
wild & mild
triangle mazes
        circles w/attitudes
disperse in fractured
levity
appellation saturation
marinating in
leisurely kill
hands tender
in ambient frail basket
strumming loudly
rowdily
indecisively
HA
out of control
vehicle
crashing
goodbye

Cove
the soaked crucifix
blood mongrel
dead eyes sleep
Stop the train
the crash is just about
keep me from getting out
Wake Up
the prison is gone
poor rodent reaching for more
look beside you
as your tongue slides out
dripping to the shiny floor
Oh, we've got trouble in us
and no one knows why
a few nails in the membrane
of one separate hand
look into the horizon
I saw it happened & kept on moving
a patriarch of Roman territory
sheets to cover the lamb
All offers refused
perimeters outside the coal mine
another instrument used

The body is found near a hot sweat groan
eyes sucked from their roots by killers
fingers crushed in the quiet streams
Phloem sap plasma, rotten mushroom
a nervous reptile eating his own tail
the length of this program is soon to fail
and all accidents will be secretly unveiled

Scenes of French regimes overthrown by cynicism
tall crude men from a different place are in the corner
conspiring acts of an evening to be stopped
the dogs are out, walking through dark alleyways
spies can neither be seen nor heard
I was told to show up early with nothing on me
part of the bar was filled w/many tsantsas
hanging on strings & were approved
by The Shuar Tribe of East Peru
everybody's faces were drawn out by the light
their voices were kept in a shy & soft tone
one of them had a glass turned over on the table
while the others dressed in wool suits
no names were exchanged
they gave me card w/one word on it

                    "Retribution"

as if it meant something

_____

We're gaining speed
it's all too close, it's getting closer
Louder, come on get it louder
pick up the speed, I want it louder
Yeah, that's right, make it good

Mayday, Mayday, Mayday we've lost control
Mayday, Mayday, Mayday, Mayday we've lost control
Mayday, Mayday, Mayday we've lost control
Mayday, Mayday, Mayday, Mayday, we've lost control
That's right
Oh, she got into town, in the middle of the night
She got into town, in the middle of the night
We picked up the speed, a place for us to hide
Away from it all, love will never die

Break the chain, we're crossing over
I like this part, this right here
It's familiar, the oldest story, what's that?
We're really doing it, I can feel this one
The waves are coming through

Constricted veins have caused abuse
In the night we all cut loose
From the things that break us down
Always near the hallowed ground

Now we try to leave this place
Often for the chance to escape
Our days are running out
Stuck behind to suffocate
Who's going to save this world
All before they change our world

Here and now, we wait around
Written on the patient's toe
Shattered glass invades the town
a jungle with no cat
forest with no trees

Crooked art tossed away
Old clocks never age
Fire burning shadows death
Lions sleeping without a threat

Special women in a locked chest
Purple hue surrounds the left
Drink the poison from the snake bite
Near the island untold, on a map

The night is getting darker
From the sun
Calling to the guard
You got a strange tide rolling
on the edge
To the other side
Passed out by the sea
We are just an hour away
Save me, from the island ahead
Somehow gone again
Looking all around
Where did he go
Calling to the guard
Calling to the guard
on the summer day
Lost in the world
of a sudden wave
Calling to the Guard

Escape once called for his name
Demanding a leap
A wish to plummet down the well
But there are many wells
With water & rocks
All alike in bucket & rope
Providing the same rain
And cold winds
And privileged air
And comfortable known
And to die in that fiery home
would said to be normal

Sit back & enjoy the show, it begins in about
30 minutes & there will be no leaving once it starts.
The ushers have even snuck away to grab a spot
behind the gallery to see what they could. Grown
men from all over the globe scavenged local libraries
to spend what little money they had left on a ticket.
Half the room is filled with important people
that've made a name for themselves. The other,
thinks they have & expect to be treated as such.
Everyone in the audience is given a metal box
with a big red button on it & are told to press
it when needed. Each night the button does
something different. On this night, one time only,
never to be repeated again, it restarts the show
with a cathartic ending for Act II & layers the
entire play off the sequela of it.

In the new image we surrender
hopelessly waiting for better
searching on our trip
we come across a ship
in the death of our hour
we summon a power
to ease the gift
like a verse never to be heard
sanctioned in its curse
open to the stars &
a pale skinned figure appears
spoken in youth as an enemy
Destroying all gates
freeing all the creatures
to unleash their perimeter
this is heritage
espionage of the first degree
a reflection to a rippled pound
strung to a child
enlightened and in-complete detention
the man was arrested to appear in the dark birth
surviving on lucid obedience of objection
an elaborate explosion aids the whisper
warning the huts of sudden outbreaks
to remove & reject an old vision
the change for Eve
roaming in the streets as shadows do
showing a talent
that could certify the glow
try the physics &
a green badge with a green jacket
will take you in &
begin an experiment

The flight of the bird is
limitless in its kind
grasping our imagination
to fill the remaining depths
especially in the
entertainment of exaggeration
Awake & you'll know the location
your inner child
the shallow land
ratified in your commitments
stuck to erase them &
convert what remains in perfect pose
this is what kept separation from
danger & evil

Revealing wishful women
across the globe
in scented image
among desert road
ruins of yesterday's village
excavated & pillaged
sent to museum shows
in full display
tickets sold w/frivoling flow
as green-eyed people
assembled mid-day
roped off in velvet strange
counting down the river's march
parting the arranged brigade
in trembling pain

For years I dwelt in the nest that reserved
the birds, Commending the wings of
· magic misfortune, teleporting insects to
fresh grave in search for simple defeat
Unearthly gloom hidden in silhouette rage
burying the forest of humble remains
a guide for divine gravity
prowling beyond the wistful nail
Charmed dance swaying the resonating sea
w/inducing success
treasuring on the gazes of spiritual aide.

I know how the universe works

Open a page into the obscure shadow
swim in wispy waters and float about
search for nothing
soon let the drown take flight
disappear with all your worries
this dim lit room will collapse & fold
into the ceiling as you begin transcending
through flashes of sketched outlines
there is no way back in knowledge

I know how the universe works

Expose your eyes it's time to understand
the quiet secret that left after the first calendar
void the teachings in holy rooms
a fallacy tethered along time
arguing with God has only crafted the wheel
there is no religion elsewhere in the mind

Rhea
search for Rhea
the adapted illusions are evaporating
melting to a grey shade where
right & wrong
good & bad
Truth & Lie
have no domain in sovereign grief
alleviating written characters to inventive conception
liberating within the world exclusive of style
absolute abyssal connecting preexistence w/existence
looking at the impossible
naked is nothing beneath it all

living as controlled conscious beings
witnessing the origins of emotions birthed
w/gritty growth
pronounced in policies of eurythmic arteries
to unify a dispensable bond in chemical attraction
inflating crafted rafts for dedication to fascination

stepping o'er unlimited promises
acceptance earned
ripping the last link of denial & disbelief
altering your foundation to hover above
the cement Earth
climbing toward undefined certainty
unaware of the vaccination
lines dividing the sidewalk
can merge
continuing the curse

divorce yourself from all branded
ideas of subconscious notion
& let chaos be your new language
let it sit in silence
peeling away the tiles
tearing the seam of nature's leaf
calling to energy
as it cuts down the walls to
uncover the unguarded meadow

clear the disorder that once sheltered you
use the same adaptation to appear
the grey shade of melted colors in restored agony
as you return to the drown
burn the page of obscure shadows and
release the restricted elements imprisoned by death
Rhea is found

Measures of time
we count you
score & record
the height grows
roses to rise
ability of rhythm
perfectly pre-tuned to the
sounds that follow
to feel existence in
your weightless gold

In his office home
With his office clothes
Behind his office desk
Doing everything told
Carpets full of smoke
Eating dinners alone
Immune to the carbons
Somewhere across
A window overlooking Neptune
Skipping breakfast
Seeing fields mutinied by dirt

Walking to his kitchen
Remembering the ode to innocence
Pouring confessions onto the couch
Clothes spilled over balcony ledge
Barring his profession to the stars
A neighbor walks out in bath robe
Hiding from an opened window

Approaching his blend to communal bow
Not sure who's to blame
Forcing the atoms to rally
Passing over
Stacking chords in the living room
Going back for one last more

Sure to keep the pot from rising
Whisky musak graduation
Invented telephones collecting alphabet
Interruption by the radio
More neighbors huddle in yesterday's scare
Wet soles glued near the monkey's cage

Offers to his rich watch
And silver shoes
Denied by covenant roots
It's far from noon
Her leather pants will soon be cool
His people will learn to love her

Now in the region of warmth
Town alarms and firefighters race
Smell of ash & tar feed the stomachs
Paris in his head
While sitting inside

Convincing the elders of safe harm
Women & children board the streets
Chained off but still shaded in heat
A birthday is celebrated
The fire would save no one
So why should we save it

Exiled from his loan
As he walks out the door
Sinking to the overture
Seats are sold and exited
Inviting the magnets to collide
Take off your glasses
And follow his lead

Follow his lead
Heading to LA
Or anywhere w/grass on its steps
Aiming for the arts
An extension of Earth
Everything else a destruction

Ruling the necessary X
All in front of him
In crescent admiration to what trails
They leave the cracked bones
Beyond the creek

Enter his forgotten childhood
Weeks spent without lie
Climbing branches to see it all
Rugs centering the room
Dinning on holiday drugs
Seeing the bugs creeping beneath logs
Memory serves well under lit candles

Cad knight of the fat sudden oasis
bathe in the empirical everglade
under epicedial crusade
the valor leads in faction resilience

upon arrival of inspection
space teeters when gruesome
lustful questions gravitate to anarchy
clowns and whistles
cars in hot pursuit

hot rodeo fever
aristocrats without reason
controlling the race
in the brute washed up shore
engaging on the jungle's heart

Feline cage
the plague unnamed
swathed fucked ephemeral
latent derision in every decision

riven lethargic burn
we eliminate the concern
enclose ourselves
to an insular return

and that's all right
to slaughter my pensive rain
warnings will soon fade
down the smokestack
and into the shade

The gentle air
her presence unaware
come to the fair
witness her stare

Tarnished silver
rotten corrosive opium
harsh sordid sailors
prostitutes & regret
with that being said
she expected a friend

Something her would unveil a union
something even more is evolved within her

motion of theater in lasting hunger
a gesture of thought to
confront the things we do
halfway there we are given an act

the longer we go
the more we try
a flue that bends weaves and turns
but in the momentum of change
we bid for a flatten disc
without chance of risk

**Centered in kites' levitation
Lies a point of two sticks
Crossed in crucifixion;
Heaven wears a thorn crown**

Strange Days

Foreign fabrics invented
                    (invited)
with imported techniques smuggled in by
pirates, crusaders, servants of her majesty, knights,
and posture of nepotism
Moreover
to teach young lovers a built city
        New York Rise
Glowing in radiant mist of numbing dullness
a poor child is awakened at night
Trading the glass hour for vacant wilderness
a deprived beast is conformed in collective fever
Standing in the façade of cogency & habilitation
our ornate mind capsized in vigil rudimentary
bought, sold & re-sold
Leaving only corpses with a mouth, but a voice
It's time to go now
we have other places to be
and meet the people who are waiting for lies
of open door love.

An eerie iridescent eco-light when riding
an external bike
parking lots submitted in dormancy
monasteries on a Monday
the shift of mood in atmosphere
that obeys malicious limbs upon
serenity of goodwill
consented & Conceited
we need leverage to strip the fray
the arc of the populous bends
in favor of the leverage
as many Tribes connect
in warrant coolly
bitter arrival tends to dissect
glorified empires & objects of jeopardy
a perfumed risk in us all
sleek ambient cavity
touching the halls
to reach new levels of modulation

stay on course
stray on course

destiny in destination
· I was drunk
tired & constrained
glinted by usual meats
the rotation amalgamated
night w/day
in uncompromised deferment
it was fun to be lost
insouciantly bewildered

The heart beats as the soul weeps as
The city cries as we tell ourselves
We're going to get by
Grab our things
No pharaoh or king or ruler
Will grab my mind
And tell me
That love is not mine

Sucking down the broken glass
cut throat, left to choke
death is slow, cold & croaked
alone far from home
picked up the hiker soaked in smoke
night comes night goes
headed to LA for the show
slit wrists and time to pass
making sure we never last
Whisky man I want another
swim too we need a few
see the blood streets up ahead
your baby's dead & covered in red
wondering if we can change
the future will never be the same

<u>Orange Hive</u>

Along came the hero to save the misfits
                        collected and fueled
he went upstairs and looked out the window
                it wasn't there yesterday but here it is
                    the cemetery arraigned & sustained
in that there was a large picket fence,
                                    (stood in spate)
                        whispering winds
the eyes receded back from where they came
                        juveniles let loose
there is a sonata that plays at the end of each year
                    and I'll be the first to ever see it
decades have given this sphere an insular regret
            causing an unrehearsed grandiosity of transient
                                    dervish ritual
supplying prominence in the twisted stars

Grabbing your hand w/the thick immobilized oil
as bubbling continues to spill over
onto simple creases in a canopy
the honored veteran sits on wood
imported from Indonesia
What happened to all the metal from WWII?
factories & hospitals consumed the nation circa 60's
newspapers got darker with each print
too much was going around
forgotten cellars shared recognitions of indigo
we stayed in the living room & kitchen for hours
building a frame with an enclosed static current
family of retained memories on which
they withdraw from
become a benevolent passerby
at the high point of Spring
it was plotting to convey shrunken observations
refused by languid curiosity
wearing bleached mockery

Migrant traveler chasing pines
across liquid flow
protecting chairs
made alike in complete black
                    w/wheels
                    & seats
gallery of animals
windowless isles
shading the delay
teachers say it's all for you
adults say it's not true
I hate christmas

The time on our side is all gone
The time on our side is all gone
I wanted more
Swimming in the sea
It was cold but, I got through

Watch you leave
I saw my baby go
She packed everything
In the night

I'm trying to get off on this ride
I'm trying to get off on this ride
One more red light
How long is this night?
Don't need to stay, on this ride

Get on a plane
Going to a place
Away from your eyes, somewhere nice

Watch you leave
I saw my baby go
She packed everything
In the night

Come on baby it's me
trust in your feet and
carry on
who will you be
come on & set me free
it's just a little while longer
oh, set me free
keeping our heads
above the freeze
Calmly in misery
Where do we breathe
when does the sea
open up
and leave
come on baby it's me

Never would I think
that it's the dock
where people crash
mourning rises in cast
it's fair to assume
that summer was
our friend
our only friend
moving out west
everyday
and it's all true
what they say
summers our only friend

It is all from the wake of a spectator
building around corners & away from
the shaken strength upon oblivious American soil
we feed lions at night
polished garden in sacred alliance
it turns to stone after a period of myrieteris
short discovery and a fusion of science & history
is temporally upheld by the citizens that surround it
protected by a covenant of philosophical sovereignty
the rest of us are waiting on a plan to test the ravine
and see where the cracks begin to spill over
after all we did dismantle an entire source of fuel

We never left this place
except for the outcome we created
delivered from a state of desperate confusion
every nite is a rejected conclusion of many
unsystematic delusions
        (evident of a cannibalistic paroxysm)

Waiting for the city to fall apart
honors & noble scholars have left
We need to destroy our vowels
we need to get mad
revolutionize our heroes
saving this lizard will take more than a handful
Albuquerque is the place to be
They got it all man
trees, mountains, jungles, so much to choose
grab your costumes
today we build my home
we make the future more clear
uncertain in the fog field ahead
there is nothing here for us

Three knocks at 5 o'clock in the morning and
every jogger on the street will be given a shovel
so, quit looking for money
everything's already been made
just pick whatever you want &
nobody will stop you, get serious
it's all monkey business
someone's going to get you
we don't need to go anywhere
there's too much fun around
you got to look both ways
before you cross over
there's no room for error
now eat your breakfast
it's all coming down
seven miles till our exit comes up
and we reach the road less traveled
take your hands off the wheel
it's the only way
our streets are flooded
w/cement barriers
that block the evidence
can you get me out of here
I got to get out of here
who's going to live after tomorrow
the ships are turning around
in front of our eyes
like the rest of them
more people are showing up
can you get me out of here

Vanity sails on hunger's relief
propelling the blades of sharp augur
to cut the lattices antidote for the willowed strand
ready to misplace the spade of canyon cadaver
in every gap, on all sides of the dice

the candidate for voyaged atlas
is under the formant of confessed certitude
granting the seasonal harvest a noose

anonymous society led to natural score
on strange computer
to not save the revised library
rebuilt in disguise of keyless entry
nothing has changed

as long as society remains
everything will pain
as long as humans sustain
everything will entertain

I perform on vague stages
singing to terrestrial rats
w/my shy voice
that extends stellar flares
whenever challenged
satisfying the soft interlude of
witnessed vacillation onto absorbed faces

denizens of labyrinth love
functioning on salient noise of
everlasting demesne above clouded parade
in radical motion

expecting the formal cake to light the
celebrated candle for fêted fetus
fueling the motors of
smoked cigars in twisted fear
as murder parallels the knob
inside ancient caverns
milking the age w/loans
of blackout memory

Nothing is sacred but her body
permanent sound echoing in dull antiquity
a dance so elegant & fine on gravel road
promising to oblivious crossroads
numbing the wool of surrendered pretend
her full world harnessed in luminous rhyme
built for the infinite time
outskirts of unanimous empire captured in
immortal seed

Oh, how she knows
nothing is pure in rue
her silent opera unspoken and true
manifesting the idiosyncrasy upon full swoon
resigning the rupture of volcanic fission
the hue of the day is haughty in her skin
influencing subjective forbearance in this
inept patroon of forward-importance

soul of her will
electrified in current veracity
as the quay of the bay harbors
scripted letters
relinquishing burden trounce to
amnesic allowance

We will not function for the pharos that wasted our
previous life. Egyptian god tracing skeletons of reptiles
making the mammoth move
in peristaltic structure of basic reward
Wanderers laced in silhouette cloth
anointed by the countenance of disrupted expression
upon the massive ritual that pulls warm sedum from
their buoyed roots. I understand with the words
you don't use, through wrought flatten pumice
Warning civilians of upscale madness
festive veil piercing any trespassers
of the sanctioned sundial
covens held skyclad in repent of our moral
onus searching for eternal youth
within the fountain or in orchestrated scheme

Blue moon
too soon
on the road
cause I got to go
won't you
come through
enter slowly &
show the ropes
I need you
tonight, all right,
follow me
we're taking flight
cookout
sun out
take your clothes &
leave your home
drive fast
through the past
always go
to the unknown
head down, grindstone
student loans &
nothing to own
tonight, all right
follow me
I got the bite

Interstellar Hallucinations:
        black nebula
        constellation collision
        galaxy precision

epochs of safe travels

Words of a leash in a cooler of despair. The rocks
race to a stifled, un-watered well. Can you hear that?
Trees fall on an open wound upon the land below.
Sunken ships seeking for revenge. The treasures of
our wealth have befriended the current. Vanity
towards the arrow inflight, cutting the grapevine,
operating on an animus glow that bury the sounds of
the cool mellow band. We lay in the unplanned, as it
havens the youth in complete subject. Gales of
smooth chaos deteriorating the antediluvian
pyramids that pharos fostered & contrived
(plotted & planned). Precisely tuned for the
numinous tavern. Meat served on opulent table,
extended from cruel perpetuity. Sit down my
Starving Artist, the river will taciturn into nihility.
What brought you here God, is it because of my
deathly trepidation? Let me finish my book, I want to
electrify your confidence. Nothing is purposely
shaped, everything a moment of appetite. Even the
mind gets tired of dreaming. Field of herders, ready
to send the spear at minute's notice. Existence is to
feed our desires, purpose is to carry our certainty.
But we don't know what's under our tongue, what's
behind the smoke room. No we can't be held for our
promises. Send the good trees to the good people,
or you can scale the wall all night long. The window
is near the ground, knock on it & she will show, all
night long. But it's different when the moon is gone,
and the lights are on. It's all about the time we play
the game. Never to lose our weekend name

Never will I understand
of this acid land
it's a trip
to take
like seas rotating
MAN
is coming
or gold
to manifest
that era of his
The miners are calling
where are you taking us?

The Painter left before he could eat
he looked around
and he threw his clothes
under the freeway
and waited

come on in
the car is full & the cigarette's burning
go now
run along
RHEA
they know who you are
but they don't know which
one you are, only pictures can
hurt.

The sniper usual and laden

the gun out in the west
the wild west
reaming the words
to shoot the day
let me fool the rock
take away his shadow & lie
exposing the killer from his
bunkered lilt

Trust The West In Her
snake hide diamond rush
everybody wants a piece of me
but I'm natures least of me
It's a strange day
& we're on our way to go

never will I look back
as I travel alone
everything saying go west
take a car west
I'm west in the west
I'm lost out of breath
I'm west in the west
I'm the west
I am
the
west
never
never rest
I am
the
west

Head N. for two days
ignore all rivers
        valleys
        jungles
        & animals

anonymous destination on portrait stilts
marveling what foreign land, we've crossed over
how belligerent bread rises when brushed w/heat
The Stars
follow the stars
what about the way of the wild?
Birds flying away
waterfalls petrified in opioid frost

Nature is South
Nurture is North

Shivla Shikwana

Tonight we lay
in our childlike
pretend
gather the
rituals and
light the tongue
with hums
of forbidden dialogue
set only to the melody
to those who hear

Sides are being chosen
How will you know what could've been?
Get out from your fucking seat
look what's around you
it's not alive
we're not alive
I just want to sleep

Give me some death
wait for no one
Kill for slaughter

let them try
let them try
I'm only one guy

Who's going to save me
Who's going to love me

You got to get off, the clouds are flying high
They're coming to take you, everyone's in disguise
You can trade it all in, but no one will stand by

Storm arrived, get behind the clouds
Storm arrived, she was looking all right
We don't know how long it's going to last
Blue sky, take it for a-ride
Blue sky, take it for a-ride
Get yourself together & come on make the night
That storm is coming down the line
That storm is coming down the line
We don't know how long it's going to last

Well I got my baby, going to love her all the time
Well I got my baby, going to get her on my side
That house of blues is nowhere in my sight
We got the whole thing going, going to save my life
That world has got my baby, going to make it right

She came in one day & I asked,
Do you want to stop by, do you want to stop by
Come meet me outside, do you want stop by

I wish I got my own, I wish I got my own
I wish I got my own, I wish I got my own

Shepherd of the so-called ranch
the modest cowboy
    the scenic route
always calm in concentration
a ghost tiptoes, open casket, embers melting
the cold grip, my deathly gesture
    in morning grip
Dreams to suffer
scared & scarred from the moonlight window
w/tensions towing my untapped wisdom
closed off fence a wooden tent
    cabins of the natural fibers
an out of control pilot stalling as he maneuvers
                in luxury jet
Will you ever learn to taste the edge of the blade
and risk your tongue from the words you waste
Is it too late to navigate through every path
with a sign & an exit
can I trade my knowledge for irony?

The definite scripture resulted in a protest
an influence of rebellion
        designated power
                the average person
Tragedy has hypnotized our decade
        and assembles a lock in our limbs
craving in the belly
        the early fires

a lovely Wooden sculpture
        made from loose soil

the government checks
        the legal threats
a cavity of expansion
        traced in weird aggression

Militant man
        deteriorating
homeward bound from
the psychics of jeopardy

Will he know what he has just done?
Will he turn around?
When the Guard of discrepancy
        can no longer read in texture,
the solider will give up his gun

Some will have blamed the pressure of air
or the region in fragrant cry
    the size of news
 awake & see where the first children
engraved the chasm of control

the great buffalo trade of the Indian wave
    cultivated from a blanket of leisure
Rehearsed in sensation
    by her natural nude

the alchemist conjures in all matter
    direct from the theory of universality
concentrating on modified vibrations
    to laminate the widows progress

passage in question
restructured translations
of old hieroglyphs
where we used to move our tongue
    in a more ancient way
one reality is more than enough
to discover our primitive crave

Jazz, the otherness
floating w/energy
untouched in the twentieth century
there was something windy in the Blues
it was outside where open casket
cemeteries never lied
sea of nostalgic bliss receded back to
a mollifying smile for a while
then a decade went by & we
heard a lasting boom for 18 years
the rest after that became integrated

Welcome my feral messengers
into the seldom fury upbeat ahead
slow & steady like the Western frontier
before the California dreamers took to LA
banishing dissonant nomads
& stubborn sons
from the city's entrance
Welcome my matrimonial accidents
it's been a long journey
between lunar and lip
let's keep our palms away
from peers and give up our
fears all our pieces that
tend to crumble when
the light is near
count the days
the bar is open all night

Save the people
and take it all
take the off-ramp
to the nearest exit
meet w/the MAN OF WAR
he's got a proposition
to buy your things
and replace them all
into eternal gifts

Fashion baby
headed to the moon
build my city
you got to heal my wounds
feel my vengeance
as I look in the mirror
nobody out here can give
you what I need
Welcome castaways, outcasts & poor hunters
this is the planet where the reward is death
joy is sex, and options are less
few have taken the trip out here
but all have been given a name
where the women are gold
the money is cold
and the thieves, and nerves actors
are stuck behind script
this is the point of no return
never leave never to be
all fantasy to the giants
and trolls that hide under the moon
limited seclusions casted upon first draw
an addict no different than a spiritual call

Back in the schoolyard when I was a kid
My father would tell me, don't give momma no lip
My mother went looking all around,
She said that child will never be found
That strange little boy, deranged with all that joy
He's going to change this town
He's going to take it down
We got to stop him now, before it hits the ground
I was feeling fine, until about the age of nine
I went inside & saw a man, he gave me some medicine,
he said "now look her child, everybody's been thinking,
you got to slow it down, stop all this nonsense and quit
messing around."
Now people I started to forget my fun
Before I knew it, I was twenty-one
The age of rock & the death of change
Then everything became so boring & plain
I got to leave this place, got to get on board
Watch myself take on all the reward
Until my great demise
I'll never wait for your goodbye

The race started nine minutes ago w/a shot
Who has my money as we cross this border?
American boy belonging to a family of credentials
preservations are requested for
occasions involving movement
blunt objects loom over the mildew
growing on areas of distinguished vigor
the closer we are to see the clock roll
the more naive our intentions become
holes dug in deserts, a full tank of gas &
a mirage is stretched out over the margins
of choreographed footprints
there's nothing else to do, at least not here

Ghosts of the great pale parade
draping the mouth
of the continental divide
ensuring secured royalties
for the heartless blind
another load of brilliant talent
unleashed upon the surreal notion
of alternant entanglement
gamblers among scientists
sapphire gems traded with
generals of false nobility
printed & prescribed to the undefinable
faces that age too quickly when prized w/levity
these were not written in a day
yet islands appear hungover

No Solider Unharmed

Are you confined in the turn of the page?
The book of words
veiled plainly on shelves above fireplaces
heedless caterpillars reincarnated in front
of our eyes, laughing at what they once
believed was home
All mistakes are precedents of happiness
I believe in misfortune & accidents
showing a heart what wanton emotion
is and was
this is the language spoken in universal code
described as flickering lights
on clouded voyage
chefs cooking w/elements of
earth, water, and air
musket soldiers bearing the rod
resonating on pious bows
tell your mysteries in lurid meditation
the inimitable Autumn storm will influence
our inherent being that centers around
aimless cataclysm lying in a regular state
of irregular change in every direction
but nobody will cease the tandem
as the first-born sights of perfected majesty
is too powerful to burden the end that is ahead

Sweet sex to
live & laugh
learn to untie
your knots;
never to unite
Broken strings
meant to blister
to clear the ends
and save
or toss
patient zero
w/a suitcase
& a plan
boarding the plane
injecting the
luck in life
where's the poison
to choose the
other side
something's going on
who's spiking
the punch
breakfast is too
early to
serve our morning meal

What is your name? What time is it?
How long are you sticking around for?
Why'd you come here? What's on your mind?

Oh, you feeling cool? You think it's all right?
You want to stay a little longer?

I should've known it was you
You took me to your room
Showed me a thing or two
Left me in your world
But I should get going baby
I should really leave the scene
Walk away from it all and
Head somewhere else
Somewhere new

I'm not asking for anything
I just want to respond, in kind

Leave it all behind

**Shame is a broken line
in a continuous stream**

Fluorescent adolescence leaping
off the highway
hitching to the real realm
shy of a map & guide
eruditions from the unknown
sending scattered seconds
of clairvoyant futures
turning iron to steel
dwelling on the conversations
of misconstrued strangers
forgetting the articles of yesterday
more huts are constructed on empty knolls
tents of nightly wool
in filament dome
prompting the literatures of ancient dales
restricting vestiges to a global entity

Prove your chaos
the 60's did it
& another
slip into the great lacuna
alluring vowels to dazed
fluttery high above Route 6
search the engines
lithe descant flavour
burnt match setting the stove
let me tell you
what only the dead know
soothsayers of the Gypsy mile
wives not here or alone
a sacrifice daintily splendored
in sifted memories
weltering sinuous currency
of notes that merge
to pages & pages of free Cabaña

Shivla Shikwana

Now is ever
Forever is now
Cut the wire let them run around
We got the plan to get ourselves out
No one can stop us
We've lost all our doubt

Take it easy, baby
    our city's on fire
The guns are waiting
    for a greedy hire
Let the Queen
    call in her soldiers
We'll take our youth
    and show them who's dire
Take me to the place of crime
Take me to your strange decline
Somethings coming for a change
We got the world in our veins

Going to get you on our side
Looking for a rebel mind

You're getting too cold, baby
Evil is in the air
The blood is dripping from your moonlight hair
Deep in the shadows with a trick up your sleeve
Gaining your power from the touch of her ease
Waiting to make another idol disappear
Our moments coming to the end of its year
Nothing can stop us baby, it's all too clear

Somethings coming for a change
Got to move for a change
Got to move for a change
Got to move for a change
Got to move for a change
Got to move for a change

Surrender right now, right now
Give up, give in, give all your things
Your days are over, baby
The end is forever
Time will take you to where you belong
Got to move for a change
Got to move for a change
Got to move for a change
Got to move for a change
Got to move for a change

Was there a day
frosted in grey
miles of lanes
calling to say
what can be told
who left the people
Now there are secrets
    riddles
    of mysteries
    that hold us in this game
you can wander in plane
unfiltered lands
but the music will grow
and the fire will stand
Come with me
I know how it will happen
when it will happen
you are the reason
of broken shattered glass
in fostered regime
the believers
of fever, and disease,
mystic circles
The totem of we
stand in tomb
to all
for all
to play
we can see
the posture of decay
come now
come all

I can do this soon
and you will be the same
so let me explore this night
before the potions save me
with their idyllic poison
Venture far
and hear the rain
the smack of pavement
that calls to command
it's a bill we're
committed to pay
And if the moon
lost its way
oh, well I'd go away
go away
go away
and never come back
to what we call safe

Here in the everything
we are full of practice
problems of remedies in reserve
happiness is not a journey
but a two-step walk out the door
embellished obsequiously in community
colors of remorse
sourced in depths of awareness
obstructed to take the detour
fasten your seatbelt
secure your permission
and lock the gate
absence is illicit
excluded to those in repair
televised or sincere

Natural sleuths for the other voice
reality is a disease
energy founded
misplaced & recycled
in order for us to be us
we must know the precincts
that embrace our corners

and if you forbid your thoughts
then let it be known
ordinary is your soul
water will fold
and regions of warmth
will begin to mold

Let's try it again but with more authenticity
give it one more shot to really make it count
who knows, maybe it'll look better
no one will be there to stop it or see it or hear it
it would feel as a hallucination in the civil poverty
of certain variations within lethargic monuments
inducing rushed rationalizations among
philosophical crevices that tend to steer towards
propagated history

Crawling in a transition where madness begins
no room for serenity only time for revolution
and the rest will continue to revolt
like an aftershock
our moral aftershock
I've cancelled the flight back home
the air is heavy
And what sober sulk
has led me to come in witness
The good is gone
the good is drawn
receive this news
a touch of power
we are heavy in this air
soon to explode
Disbelief & doubt
the long way
my only way

She's a tall glass of water at night
She's a tall glass of water at night
Taking everything in sight
Breaking all the rules to fight
She's a tall glass of water at night

Full of heart, on a rainy day
Near a bird of prey, got to come away
Coming to contain, what love remains
I want to change it all, our sign on the line
Will you wait for my legs to walk

She's a tall glass of water at night
She's a tall glass of water at night
Taking everything in sight
Breaking all the rules to fight
She's a tall glass of water at night

Classic Blues
3rd to electrify confusion
terminus of words
Prince of Madoc
releasing the folk
that fled dominate raiders as
New mediators
render the loss of hope
connected tensions tabulating
Itinerant fission
bonds of the ally
covenant amusement
second to first
last of the Earth
prepare your dough
the guest of the castle
have architect tracery in the
environment they stained

Like the idols of tapestry to fend the gloom,
an accent received in the nipple of news.
a message on ink:

"it was never the night that left us in rue,
   the flood was full, and sky was blue"

───────────────────────────────

<u>Totem</u>

Naturally under the spell of spin
young & edgeless, symmetrically tuned
the motion imported from deep within
a spotlight for the creatures of dark
an eternal loop to pure simplicity
untaught but known
instinctively drawn, redrawn
learned by our fellow moon
a totem adapted for the wheel
overlooked by the fruits we peel
churches we kneel
clustered in dots
and scratched to reveal
planets, atoms, and asteroids
intertwined in the unified meal

Cursed in the mind of a poet,
an abnormal truth further beyond the desk.
An answer so obvious yet denied, must be kept.
It's so dull to understand it all.
To know the lies told by religion, people, & our eyes.
A gift pertained to gain for what you really want.
And the answer remains the same for all poets w/out
shame, fear or pain. The ones who speak in favor of
their tongue, greeting the crowds to question him.
I figured it out long ago, long before my words
were written. You can ask away but the poet in me
will leave everything dazed. A talent so useless when
strained. A compass w/out needle or North, has
led me in surface in the midst of my search.
Now I end the hunt, knowing the maze.
I am left in the middle,
between lunar & lip
I am a captain without ship.

1st night of sonata has linked the stage
to stop a rower in his track
laughter is its own form of seriousness
the ovation is surrendered to women
of freedom I like to believe the captured
an ode to Wilderness
I'm sick of this ride
before I puke over the balcony
and get ripped from my seat
(after all I did pay for my ticket)
thrown outside and left on the street
Just give me a nod &
I'll do it again
broken walls & chairs
people who are afraid to be
and grown men weeping in suits
I want to be free
I want to be now
What life is mine if I cannot choose
the voyager in me has had enough

Actors left to stand
fathers in preservation
doctors turn rooms to cold
teachers stuck in school
levers unsullied
by the worker in hat
to live a profession
is a performance of itself
with a stage of itself

The play is nothing
without the orchestra
the fields are empty
without the animals
sleep is plain without sex
a king is cruel to the oppressed
our connecters merge
when mental seclusion is in affect

The trip on the highway is
joined by Cities of loud leaders
in full say of their verse
Government rule can parish
in the arms of the irritant
My voice can speak for itself
Restricted by rules and
set of decrees
is not a work in progress
Escort me from this venue
and let the friends of my life
decide their future

        You are only free
        when you can pursue
        all your desires without
        (specially) self-judgement

let the rumors of death spread
in wildfire
Angel from heaven
take me away from this rest
away from this polluted atmosphere
we currently nest

A lifetime of people have casually
been caught in the net of submission
there is nothing more potent than
a knife near rope
high above it all
Seven days can split our love
My final wish will to be to give it all away
to the Rock & Roll stage

I can see the masque from my hill
forest webbed in silk infancy
as the stars of the underground are shot
back into orbit by the serpent's will
we will never need to accomplish anything
but of our own decency
Inn the laughter of cotton treasures
full thoughts will dance forever
I plan on my being of innocence
to carry me from leather seats
to leather pants
the world is full of hints
and trophies to gift
But not for me or my life
that is mine
When the clocks are tossed
and time is lost
everything will deem ordinate
in season & color
arriving without need
or violence of law & rule

In rebellion of this all is a bounty
Set by my neighbors when they were
just as me.
The universe of my soul is restricted
to only the echo of what can't be seen
our perception of our past has
led you to deluge your primal nerves
and cause a myth
in true nobility
I will not take part in the
grievance of sorrow
my structure of lunacy
is not of nature
nor of man
tied by my arms in bound
of the creature that
once lead me to valley
further than existence
I awoke in the jungle
naked & free

Rooftop girls dance on the solstice sleep
invading the avenues & sandy beach
it looks so empty when streets turn off
let's sneak onto the shore
& perform wicked songs
under the spell of cheerful laughs
toss our innocence into the flames
summer wears our true signs
taking us to latter heights
never to leave or bleed or end
the anniversary of our toppled walls
a demise of forged flames
delivering the infinite day
upon the 12th hour
the atoms are w/us tonight

-Who is that over the hill?
What do you want with me?
I called upon you
-How am I supposed to get in?
she has the key
-Where you're going,
there are no doors
-Who's to say I want to stay?
                    Maybe

-It isn't where you think
you're going that will ease
your mind from hesitation

-It's where you hope to be going

Let me tell you about the road,
the road to Heaven
the one w/lights &
how it starts on the grassy knoll

_____

Water strikes his face in the late hours of May
the empty bank, closed off for improvements
not to be reopened for another six weeks
What are they doing in there?
How long does it take to get new tables & chairs?
I've had bones heel faster, not mine though
100 years will have gone by &
mirrors won't be different
spoons will be used in the same manner
as they were built for
belts will still go around the waste
the wheel will still be round & roll, maybe faster
but sound rules them all
this nature will produce the same noise
no matter how much we conquer

Shivla Shikwana

Radiant waves in supple surgery
trending the new generation
to observe all others
before turning around
and heading bravely
A full spin has before unwind
ignoring the up & down
that had never explored

Enjoy the victory
humble yet respite
strong rasping virulence
Sweet mongrel
        textile sleuth
lawless women the littoral embroidery
igneous coal sodden husk
take it upon yourself
to not enter the optic slumber

gruesome Corners colliding
sheep rustle through the farmland
gothic range
permanent residency
an alternative solution to age w/out time

a direct line from primordial oddity
presaging antecedent evanescence
Porcelain neck, iridescent Satyr monolith
show me the survivors
the ones in desperate care

Broke bandit running from action
Take an army away from practice

Follow it all into its all
empty the bottles &
clear the clouds
water the plants
full of true wickedness,
religion & doubt
an enemy to the shrewd
croon of old hum
Shaman monk in pale robe
planting the kernel to the next
Venda Cycad for our
native ceremony

Now let's study the movements of the ancient ones
the children begged and the adults forgave
a mild disbelief can alter the atoms, the bombs & stiffen
the confusion into an unusual scent
It was right in front of our eyes
the poles were disguised and
I was the first to admit the knowledge in tuned
a note was sent to me before the 3rd shift

"can is more powerful than will"

stable in the dirge coffin of flowers that express
the story of everything beautiful
we ignore those notions & linger on
we choose our conscious, but the stars aligned
chooses the frequency of their luminous shine

Rest in the field where royal tensions spry
babies and old fools crawling
taking their time
penetration through the skin
a message received
(a hint perceived)
have you spread the stroke
where can I meet you at this late hour
I want to hear it all
let's relocate the organisms
to ceremonial Neopaganism
redefining our eternal sanities
in copacetic insolence

Peruvian basket
history woven to its galore
incorporated melody
a tonic of murmurs
the token to traditional remedies
polished for abled norm

Time after the saga we sit and wait
like the spiral snake that slithers & flakes
we participate to stay awake
under the whispers
the madhouse is ours
we took it over after every chance the Malibu
weather was out in our favor
planned & performed for the dwellers that reside
Customary cultures
hardship hope
extrinsic identity

                    it came & went
                    from one station to the next

something was after us in the woods
we were being chased away
turned around and gave it one last look
it had claws of rape
cunts and cocks pushing the branches
faster we ran into the cave

we heard a noise
it was warm & mellow

slick and sly sealing our doom
the air was drawn out
we came to our senses & recalled
what grew on the farmers land
what rained on the mountain side
we slipped deeper into the cavity
contemplating which foot took the first step

I looked ahead & saw a light we were almost there
safe in the poverty of chance
she ran with joy
faith was wrapped in velvet magic & none of us
were hurt harmed or hindered

Gently into the horror of pain there is no evil
creatures of pleasure smirk to agile limbs
that twitch when fear is supplied
a kind of insanity has made its
way to our supple brain
deviating the course of action that follows

> we used to lead a charge of liberated drama
> we came to music for wicked indulgence
> to sacrifice nothing
> it was all fair equal & solidified

and then the groove came on & we were with it
starling white clouds came to greet us
we were stuffed & had no room for anymore
I asked but we had already entered the residence
of newborn symmetry

Somewhere in our preexisting lives they are
filled with aloof unconfiding coincidence
that give lift to elusive irony
making it difficult to notice

The Trip Continues

Shivla Shikwana

days are a blessing
decades are a curse
feet are a gift
bones are a nightmare
young is a promise
old is a story

Here in the heavenly tune it all comes together
it's rueful and mystic like the
hardship of heroism we can't deny
we choose the night in its tranquility
it's soft & menace
no mercy has ever bestowed upon those
who've fallen from its shelter
limiting our souls & locking our minds
there is no escaping where the dead have died

what made the gods leave us behind?
was it war & crime?
what brought the universe back to our lives?
was it music & rhyme?
So it was told & constructed
and we traded our eternal sty
for blissful waves that help us fly
further into depths of her canvas
she forges a new fabric
a new cloth
made of freedom
we named the things we love
to know the things we hate
we kept our image
no longer for us to wait
marching on the streets
towards the hum of strange

rawhide

the big city flooded in forgotten cry
no one was around, and I lit the ghost town
to start a new constitution
the beaches were our priceless jewels
our outside clue to the soles of our shoes
parades cultivated in prehistoric promise
trapping the hills to a monsoon of vibrant prolixity
                    scarecrow mints
                        glass hammer
                            turning dials
or tendril seed
sylvan cupola
I've seen a lot of things
I've seen the architects change the world

Hotel residents amplified in realm
varmint liquor introducing sullen loop
in the frequency of the captain's gist
that controls the strange mercy of
the ocean's calm

blue sky's blink near infant days
dressing the wound as the sun bathes
a cooked meal polluting the famished
pirating the isles of Mischief Allocation

industrial winds instructing the cloth
posture of paradise
parades & politics
in the chime of a beaten bell as quiescent toddlers
journey into lunar connection

Portland railroads heading East
destination set to the garden of Eden

warped in tropic bliss
the Alaskan dawn on winter's shrine
eating hot soup & dreaming of the
misplaced needle

why would I let this happen
two doors down from her quiet abode
mourning the night away
backyards will never be the same

More for the trees that holler
it wasn't too long ago when we
saw the theater in its prime
the cool vacancy that it would uphold
      keeping the Latin charm firm under her arm
Because of this reach we abort the blood
to fill the creek
he is frayed apart from all limbs
breathing w/only one rib
alone in the desert scene
violence has caused the scorpion

(a tattoo inside the membrane)

to rogue his fellow reptiles
into geometric confinement

solitary is a daunting habitation
one where you're sure to suffocate
come on everybody's doing it
and nobody's stopping it

I don't know
no, I don't mind
the world is fine
and so am I

Dark miles of picaresque
cosmic range set in its paradigm
the judge is blind like it should be
I know the words to his speech
recite my vows like the Monks did
We used to feel casual in our clothes
but now we are elasticated for the time being
who will start the engines to get us out of here
well looks like we lost our ticket
this is my new palace & it's flooded in bitterness
some say it wasn't horrible but others
others say the relics were the first to roar
baking the wine
blood in the teeth
what did you eat? Was it flesh?
So let the hanging of our sparrows
and wild bulls begin
their death is only a sacrifice
don't you remember this was in the book
shouting w/a verrucous echo
the place was disgusted & we got kicked out
back on the streets little one
kid of the kings
garbage in the streets
HAHA more for me
serve the soup
for we are all hungry today
this marks our grave
right here on this idiot land
my soul is with me

Aluminum box along the webs
sweating in the stuttering lane
ignorant shadow beneath her yarn
in wedding ceremony
collecting the debt of
                    fur coats & constructed caves
French heroine in perfect tilt of Saturn's ring
frostbite venom in poisonous persuasion w/the
hitchhiker of the locked cabinet

                                (5 minutes remain)

yellow paint dripping on the tiles
into the baby's throne & animals
began to moan
I am the Lion tamer

mental illusions are not my enemy
odd numbers begin to fade
and the brain will send a wave
through dry, odorless scent
prepping the schoolyard kids for
televised news on channeled passage
favoring the hint of idled fashion

142

Climbing down a hole
Looking for some fun
Trying to take it all
Just grab your gun
Let's get lost
Right now, come on

Signing to a deal
Body on the bed
Losing everyone
for a shot in the dark
Just grab your gun
And, let's get lost
With me

Lost, baby
Lost, baby
Lost, baby
With me

They don't have to know where you've been all along
Stuck in the show like a fly on the log
Your mind is going to be auctioned off
Before you know it, you'll be lying right there

People in the town want to go real far
They're getting in a moving car
Not slowing down, here comes a brick wall
The next day it goes again

Lost, baby
Lost, baby
Lost, baby
With me

Whatever happened to the great mistake
The one that got us to plan an overtake
A bell cannot ring in the sway of the wind
Too much weight, and it won't go

Now the smoke is starting to clear
The road is long, we're changing gears

Here it comes
No more time
All for one
One for none
It's all over

Philosophical solider in red shoes
tasting the hallows of denial
delusion is a disease dissected on demand
surgical solution pollution
laminating ghouls, goblins & gnomes
Phantom spine to bend a way
to leave the yard
& mold the rage

    Motown strangers on the back of the bus
    severe scavenge sought inside the cusp
    mechanisms slowly turning to rust
    skeptic reliever supplying his lust

go outside and take the call
down the steps into the mica cavern
later they'll be used as countertops
diluting a harsh cadence in the kitchen
and then you'll appear right in front
of the fall wasting your seconds
before it happens once more
waiting in line
or deciding a lie
the vendetta has worn the mask
                choices have been made

Dormant lullaby
caught in the center
of the interstate tulip
reason to deem the judge
in the amp of the chords
a flavor lasting for good taste
separating blood cells
from plasma
they look for written sheets
expanding the calicoes to fit
around the bend

it has spilled all over the tiles
in many forms
and many colors

revolutions of cyclized planets
incessantly gamut inside the seekers telescope
chimney smoke assembled in politics
as it crawls to be outdoors
go outside
and be a part of the rich oxygen
feed the trees your noxious grasp
filtering the calm w/brewed breaths

And she was afraid
of it all
shouting to be saved
from it all
there were moments
poured rays
tempted sands
a posed memory
always undocumented
greeting the robes
w/a tangled belt
her bedroom laced
by crumbs of rigid corrugation
now panic as you melt
in a puddle of erupting ash
all to be lost in appliance
welting w/unheard methods
as everything stares back at you
testing all of you at once
leaving only a shattered mirror
or a prostrated branch

Shivla Shikwana

**We were soothed by promised surprises
upon fragile disguises**

Strange Days

Shivla Shikwana

Letters to my girl
we're going somewhere exotic
O, you know my soul
you're my anecdotic
falling to your spell
what brought me here to you
I could never tell

searching for the heat
serving your detention
walking to your beat
we all have our obsessions
invitation to cession
obligated confession
never learned your lesson

in the planned parade
O, baby say
what you have to say

don't go away
please come & stay
O, baby stay

until the day spins the other way
we won't be here to save
coming down the strange
unsullied lane
calling to our name

and on that day we'll meet again
but until then just send a way

another day
another day
another day

There must be risks of casual tendencies
we need betrayal of emotions
we mean to harm those that slow us down
there are borders & gates in each of us
the ones that hold values in our grace
come toward the true mistake
a masterpiece of splattered paint
wherever you want to go
this shape proclaims nothing
seldom in our search have we been
reasserted w/gratitude or regret
salt wounds
the creed of bliss
ripped from those who
were taken from misstep
give up slumber
give up concentration
the marrow of pressure among the gravity
Will it be too much? Is it not enough?
Can I continue to dine in constant pleasure,
as steam jubilantly exports the meat served?

Remember when we
resigned from our hands
I haven't felt anything sense
my steps have done all
the walking for me

excursion so mild
a touch of feel
coming down the steps
the suitcase is packed
& I'm ready to go back home
I've forgot my name and all
the things I could've possessed

<u>On The Run</u>

Tell me about my baby
She looked so good, she's on my mind
All through the night, in the afternoon
Going to make it right, going to love her soon

I'm ready every night, I'm ready all the time
Got to make it last, start on something new
Look around, take a check
Come back, all right, baby

As she walks down the street
Waiting at the door, for me
You want to come over here
Have me set you free
Want to get on board
Save you from the scene

Just a little while longer now
Till I love my girl
So, let's keep on going
And get me on the move

On the run, on the run
On the run, on the run
Only way, someday
Real fast, real soon

No one was around to slow you down
Never lost, always found
Got to make the night, all the way
Everyone is gone, they left in the morning breeze
She wanted to stay, pushed me off the train
Took me on a ride

It's just us now, no one else
Only us, all alone

It's getting real good
Put yourself on the news
Put yourself on a map
Put yourself on the screen
Get the whole world watching you

Let them come by with rage
They're going to waste all their time
Let them try to say

Baby, they can't stop your good thing
So, get it all, let's keep on going
And get me on the move

On the run, on the run
On the run, on the run
Only way, someday
Real fast, real soon

Don't need to hold it all back, come on

The circle of time in ruins of Aztec shrine
gold walls hidden with remedies of incense
brick by brick the bastion crumbles
decorating the citizens market
free-will is transformed into simple facility
and the crops die one-by-one
starving the stipple portrait
evaluating our ether as a morbid
                essence to fortitude

Forgotten alphabet
of bright young risk
to use my scathed
real face
jaw aligned in narrow spar
hair long to conceal the norm

    -looking around
    the classroom
    -seeing the lungs of
    every reason

There are two eyes to every face
    one is good
    the other, true
flipping the world upside-down
to balance humanity
as it should be
according to us
Sponge filled books
act normal
    as people do
blend in
    like nobody knew

Feeling so open between cocks' crows
we will exist in completed
full thoughts
like a lion's roar

Spending the loot to command the fleet
is one way to go about it
the others:
> bribing the officials
> stage a mutiny
> bury the plunder

and the warden won't accept a request
but will entrust the key to one chest
> > > body & bone
brilliant isn't it?
To give the wind a sail to blow on

Do you like disorder when it
arrives on a silver platter
gold glass,
forks,
knives,
Scotch bourbon
in the isles of Indian fires
served to say the least
to salute the saloon
bartender bringing a new glass
to pour a drink of the past
staggering demons to the next step
My brain has something to say
keep down and hear
what it has to say:

    "hundreds of miles
    long innocent piles
    boneyard treats
    corridors of carpets
    repeat
    shovels are only used
    for one thing:

        to bury"

A prey and his stray captured
along the fine sought out rain
it's a long erotic cycle
satisfaction is a game
entertainment intercepted to the creature
that can take it by the stick
everything is gone in a smug smile
so the look upon me is rubbles of disco
Pick me they said
I'm here they said
get it while you can and
maybe you could climb the snow
with a bootstrap and a coat
and everything would flow
or not flow
long as they be as what we've declared
then how can we alter what we aren't sure
the cancer of Love

When the ill troubles of the black night
can't render a simple day and
all the life in conversation is conspired
rip the consent from the aborted mercury &
let the fish drown in the pause of its death
final meal
awkward appeal
delivering each ounce of agony in every sip
calescent misery in dark frenzy
piranha paradise
feeding the gambling man
twisted in piano wire & absorbed by the sea
waves drunk and angry
the decision has been made to take us to foul

We crucified
we came to inspect
but in the end we left it for dead
hesitating w/a merriment stroll
worshiping the falsely accused

unusual
bounded
sullen

a width of imitation in the myths
tearing down the kingdom
crushed for a shortcut to understand
Who wants to rely on crossroads
raw legions in exile
forest of season
retire to your show
Left to play without
challenge or contest
bring in your best
don't let it sting
give me a little clue
unburden the run
and that's crap

Scent of a beast in the cripple mind from what it eats.
Relinquishing the flesh from a cruel burn where the sun
beats. Reformed inside the guts that fill w/meat.
Walking along & taking a drink from the creek,
while the blood still leaks.
The breath of the beast in complete reek,
no one can save where this man
last screamed & shrieked.
The supervisor in utter freak.
The people unable to speak.
One by one they silently sneak,
out from the den & into the violence.
Lost navigation that led the natives out,
and we bask in its burial ground
wanting, expecting, the medicine.
To see the room of this creature
pursing a sensuous tune,
as we come closer in its captured pain.

Hello my infested fog
creeping along the flat plain
crossed legs
casual in conversation
intellectual insects forging a canoe
tales of dramatic interlude
enter the mood
among the soup
that boils before stewed
served in cups of empty linage
as we are getting through
I lived above ground

Red lights paused circulation
speed borders directing corrected lanes
stripping cool genetics
from original development

melted glue
webbing the food
sinuating gothic jewels
frightening the loud thunder
that proceeds w/lightening

nomadic motion
KENETIC
two wheels is all that's needed
large knoll
and protected path
sticks w/useless spikes
no one is free

it must be sent
in sores
and slits
    of sperm needles
packing in the hotel fridge
blink twice
abled hands think alike
taking a composed note
in mutual share
park benches
providing beds for
feathered joints

sip the mug
in tired adoration
dreams don't last
in graveyard stones
area codes
zip codes
postal codes
hidden codes
everything secluded
born to be ruined

Well the watch is ticking
moving in delicate motion
timing all the things we do
creating rushed esteem
stage filled w/humble adorers
the band played in old attire
the ink in minted surprise
locked car
minerals huddled in coupled wood

fossils uncovered
decrypting traces of garnished gravy
evidence
Fingers twined
strands of muscles
loving my girl
my unearthly girl
she can do anything

LAkeside knife tangled in disbelief confusion
trimming the edges of crusted hope
in directed abjuration leaving behind
dense buoyancy in the crib of infancy
polarized in posed pictures
& absconding the routine of
Coffee cup crow
Determined to list expiration dates
of shared digraphs
the idiot dweller earns hills on Highway 46
unplanned mirage the sentient sentiment
of western saloon to lizard lagoon
rounding the final herd of dawns shadow
finalized in one syllable
Potent pulp ceasing Vietnam leaf
in which the lone flag inhales on the popular tales
of Windstream breeze
summers gathered in précised deed
& riddles of lucid awakenings
stroll to casual ambiguity
of airport traffic

Will you ever deliver
    all of your good love
Can you ever consider
    what we flew above

No I never broke our promise
        or found a new home
It was right in front of us
        the moon that we owned

Taken us to a new time
    you were always on my mind
I made it to the graveyard
    in our restless
        sought lives

We could
    Sense our
        Remorse

But in the end it'll be gone
        and we'll
    Never have another course

In the time
in the time
    masked in disguise
lies, spies,
    Baptized in surprise

Now I'm wandering from the
    crossroads they meet
A stubborn individual
    shadows on the street

It could fall in all directions
   our midnight intentions
Can you ever look back
        and forget
        our Connections

The last little game
   we hope to play
A chance to spend it
   all in one day

Before we come
    to the
      End of
        our ways

Artic Wolf bursting from the icecaps
chasing the distance w/each claw he lays
while a blizzard reaches the tundra to fame
a loss of coordination from the faint glint flame
nature has conducted its serge of synthesis
                    (the fabric of whole)
and we watched like salient observers
as the storm took its course
he has gone long enough to deem the den
Whichever way he goes he'll still be able
to escape the snow

Heaven, Hell, Prayers,
Slaves & Truth Sayers
nomads, bad guys &
their lustful wives
Women bored
Women adored
reality suspended
the TV intervention
vibrant milk
she woke up at noon
& was carried in silk
the weather spoon
that took her to June
Later the 20th century
in bright colour
no longer will we need
wine to muller
Obscene bars
the Satyr in charge
a leopard to starve
the Queen is full of fat
& killing the rats
Footprint soil
trails of Indians
The Native Man
in his eternal cloth
Tobacco farm
my drunken charm
The Velvet air
suspended in our affairs
Our murky swear
the promise we dare

Graveyard roses permitting silent wars
the midnight spoor filled w/stunned galore
broken glass argues the entrance
nursing the humble fruit to breed
calling for a different day
we still can cross the bridge
we still can cross the bridge

trust the west in her
the last words she will ever say
to the dunes they pour
a picture to be framed
only eyes can capture

Sounds of color
tangs of a feel
sent on a trip
through the nerves
of a soaring signal
stopped by the scent
only to follow its way back
designed to ring through our body
w/ intense stolen rapt

Atlas map interrupting
illusory lines
the first thing you see
in outer space
is an ocean
getting along w/other oceans
wrapped in the underlying
cotton arms of strict formation
mimicking the mountains above

enter the caves in vigor aura
withstand the vast array
of delicate purl
loaming dust
wiped w/rags
to see the suffer

exposed in the shattered
constant fur of soft perimeter
rolling around in the fields of grass
I woke up to acquire an absorption
of stripped life & scattered youth

_____

Who can tell me where myth began
Stiff skin in scared silence
progress among the symbols
the cool eternal symbols
deep lashes inside the dry journey
talk among the ages
in mass hour
claim to connection
claim to wisdom
cling in broadcast for
reinvented self-declivity
as we mineralize our
divine envy along ancient grounds
tall protected flowers
in our kept music
playing loudly
release the animals from
their cages & slaughtered
destined fortune
deliver a thought in unmarked
hesitation
we've done this before
left to die after the first night
after the first month of the moon
or so they say
Keys of united lust
giving us joy in silk road
miles of constructed highway
reborn in slow cackling virtue
filled w/fleeing souls
kind cruel blankets laid
on top of brute sounds

to sleep at night is
to miss half the show
shaming our own species
for naturalistic behavior
of subjective emergent sensations
upon our programmed cells
new rules of free insanity
her thigh captured mortality
as if nothing were around us
we need elder streams
shared rich copulation
leading plastered attitudes
in the creation of art

The museum is about to open
a showcase of mutants & three-eyed freaks
these instruments w/no musicians
sent off to be seen but not touched
sacrificed in the cool perpetuate punch
of our hand stitched cotton membrane
inside the silk algorithm that transforms
rough scales along the façade to be worn
as a luxurious imported fabric around the neck

Where we agree more w/a crystal ball
resources are scarce for each individual
the horse & the desert
the cowboy in boots
miles of unseeded land
the cavern night
come shower in the waterfall
the underwater earth
jagged along the bed of the shore
crabs & shells fill the floor
a vault to keep the brush from drying
and like a flash of light that quickly
calls to darkness
somehow the fireplace fills the home

Engraved on the
side of the basilica
past the first colonnade
toward the east side
where the dome
apse can be found
ensures an easy passage
to a labyrinth beneath Paris
Stick to the guide fella
it gets really dark in here
These antiques are
centered around the
condition of their age
Situations may arise
when the fog disappears
& the sheep wander away
from their safe zone for
the coyotes to claim as
their snack. If anyone is
going to Madre, it's me
I have a few things
I need to pick up from
the hospital that's not
found anywhere else & I'm
not talking medicine fella

Metal strips of thin copper wings. A pilot's
position is to operate above the sea. Melted
magma strapped in the slope of the mountain
& flowing through the modern world. The
violin stroke, a lesser calm for a simple tune.
Renewed in ceremonial subscription, a presence
awaits. A mild spice added to our bowl. The
howl of the Hound. Bravery enlisted upon a
singular breed, a sure test in the flight of a stream.
Full aware of her stubborn breeze, grown
to claim an illustrious sound that recognizes
her willful words. The push for pleasantry
in royal latitude. Stellar uncut night, washed
away for our eyes to petrify our connecters that
evaporate upon the light that answers. An isle
of clues we restlessly learn to form. Stroked &
medicated, our swim in the blues shrugged off
to a traditional malice of eager intentions. We
expect fur in fashion but receive a stain in time.
Somewhere in our illusion an addiction is
gripped & held to stretch out the day.
Room for more in this great offer we chose.
To chase her charm in this game for hire.
Fractured w/temperature in the words we repeat,
a large portrait above the mantle, tilted to
imperfections. The leather curves in her
wicked ways, laminated for the Earth to frame.
I know where to sleep on this late arrival.
Leave in peace or cause a commotion, it takes an
echo to hear the past. A drop of rain falls and we
look up. To swim in season and leave a mess.
This hive we've trapped in our broken branch
& buried beneath the milieu to protect what we

hold in the safe that we close. Contenders all
around, dressed in Southern hospitality to
unwrap a language. Spoken from a greeting into
consciousness. Skulls in the attic, rats in the walls.
I drink the wino w/out limits or reality. Clean
air flows to flood above the tides, a fresher
breeze in preserved pander. Concealed sirens,
a smile unfolds, the Envy of gold. Run far by far,
thrill of quality to the outlaws left. Much of this
was a dance inside the pale wet forest. It gave
violence a new danger. Haunted w/laughter,
still laughter. Sudden battle born in panic, darkness
forgotten & misplaced. I've left fear from my
face in languid psychic pose. Her style was
challenged, it brought gesture to mockery. The
struggle removed what little indirection progressed
in certain hope. Do you know the wisdom that's
wasted on her? Do you know the symbols
inscribed in the caves? A knock is heard & we
slept through the night. Let's find action before
the silence of death. Make loads of discoveries &
embark on a chance for change. Cattle hide shoes,
runway strip, my gentle croon, mad w/miracle.
Surprised in sylvan cracked fire, the slaughters
assembled w/philanthropic creed. Nightmare love,
champion rider, set aside from reason. We are
bandits by decree, roaming from rivers to islands.
Streets are filled w/avenues, midnight girl. The
wait for warmth, await in order, opportunity is
reflected. Arise my girl, take your time.
Perform your act & deliver the great feast to our
fragile lustful lives. Space mandala, show a voice,
invade them. Reinvent the wonder. Fight the

in-between we protest in moments of boredom.
Numbly ensconced to an attraction w/motion,
a little risk goes a long long way. Verge of village,
fluttered clouds, rested in secret literature. Searched
the naked meadow. Step toward a complete
sound, narrow from nurture. There was an intense
victory over the rustling trees. A morass arrangement,
merging softly beneath an open middle. The
drunkenness fear fed from bewildered musk. I
can operate w/in the news, to glean w/horror &
depart from survival. We are necessary neighbors
for monstrous scars. Her swift exile into the
eternal plane. Crippled city torn as she guides the
politics of luxury. Fathers flushed in tell of their
story, such embroider, touch of skin. Our ambient
wealth leaping quietly like angels reaching for help.
Where imagery speaks pure negligence and utters
desire, the control to nothingness is propagated in
a wild child. The favor given again & we wait
around & compete w/mere infinite courage. Picked
for pork, enchanted year, awake beside a remnant
calm. Soon the velvet breath is seen in classical swirl,
bitter stallion, alone desert. Let wisdom be the final
sleep, a perfect plenty into the endless dance.

Shivla Shikwana

I wait for the elevator to rise
this is the worst stairs I've ever walked

I'm waiting on a war
a worried elaborate hand
our famous journey ends

Another candle burns again
will it be what we see
a night of mystery

Rhea well alive

Evening stroll
rampant roots
footprint trail
sparked in youth
The one act show
in late afternoon
such heavy crown

You've valued your
inner being into a
conception of
rhythm

I can offer something
new & benevolent
Far fervor
center of action

Shivla Shikwana

The calculous dream
of great lengths
An ivory gem
taken w/
every instinct

Neon
mirror
entropy riddled
patient

A palliative lie
the fragrant air

You met the goddess
sweet Dionysus
heaven born witness
and it was you

Scarlet rage
fragile loam, streamed ravine

I arrived w/nothing
electric current
The roundabout

Stuck in this circle
from your first trip to Arizona
near a broadcast
it was written on a napkin

Shake waste
Rhea

The verdict is in
an innocuous pension
or give it all together
satan's wish
so it to be surfaced
levelled off
& assumed

Morphine missile
the citizens in liquid luck

I called w/experience
haggard yet inventive
Unplugged to my location
an utter familiarity revealed

The resonant bell
a full-throated siren

Send your love to me
I need your love today
Send your love to me
Come on, meet me halfway
Send it all baby, yeah one time for me
Send your love my way

Drawn to the night
No time to waste
The wars we fight
Turn up misplaced
Untold where to go
Send your love to me
Won't you make it so

I need your love today
All through the week
I need your love baby
Your heart's a mystery
Yeah one time for me
I just want to stay
Send your love my way

Send your love to me
I need your love today
Send your love to me
Come on, meet me halfway
Send it all baby, yeah one time for me
Send your love my way

Goodbye sleep
It's time to leave
No one will see
What we believed
Right there, in front of our dreams
We came so close
But left it all in a scream

One shout
One place to go

Let our love die young
And we'll never grow old

What a perfect tragedy
That lives inside me

Send your love to me
I need your love today
Send your love to me
Come on, meet me halfway
Send it all baby, yeah one time for me
Send your love my way
Send your love my way
Send it all today
Send your love my way
Send it all so I can stay
Send it all my way

The interview invokes upon us a system
of checks to modulate our manifestation
devoid from reaction
a chemical combination
Beneath the elaborate labyrinth is an older
organism of an even more impossible index
prolonged w/adamant recantation
a family of native inception is tricked &
trapped in the lattice of its scheme
Serpents tail whipped & veiled
the beginning to a loss is an end to a gain
a simple truth but a truth no less

There is a muddled Fire within my soul
I figured it out one drunken night
alone & gone it had been buried
so deep that it was masquerading
as a Zen filled man a peaceful contender
Troubled to my validation I revealed
a curious bungalow
when completely released I gripped
to its allure & embodied the form
as my own as it was my own
I saw something outside the shade
of calm & reason
a Rebellion to society from its operations
to be able to change the world
Cautious of violence & menace there is
a Shaman healer of pure sagacity within
the cells of my blood
Confidential to my swayers
I made a choice like every compromise
to settle in-between the lines
as each day became a part of the past
it was welcoming more fuel to my blaze
controlled & fortified for the first time
I now wait on a certain day
to cause change away from violence
all for the fun of the game

For the sake of argument where all things cruise
the underbelly of boats shine with gold mockery
disturbance in her waspy reflective pool
the Orange avenue
                                    the lunch room
gained meats on our legs & arms
St. Valentine drugged the youth from palms apart
how we were naïve to run our hands through her
earning the distance instead of capturing
her existence how many of us will it take
                        we were rich in each other
girls in suits took off their shoes
they went to the store for nothing more
Alone with a scene
Veterans in green
a shot of ecstasy dripping from syringe
astronauts, sappers, scrap metal,
our toys in the attic
our instruments abandoned
to sit not stand,
to laugh but cry
to wonder but why
our curious spy to fill the sky

Cave drawings have startled the Mutants
they are sages of stories, tales, and confusion

Vibrant and contemptuous upon setting the mood
an evocation to paintings that's sure to come soon

First of the virtuosities to settle the score
but where they came from is riddled in the core

Fixed in display never to touch time
like heroes upon war breaking the line

We will be a secret society of nimble compunction
adoration embedded deep within seduction

Everything our eyes can kiss is fair, true, & ripe
leaving ships to dance on the waves at night

When the room is empty, and the piano is strong
the image will disperse, and nothing will wrong

Speaking to foreigners in native rule
without the use of words or tools

Who will crack the code that is the arts
a shaman monk or a spiraling dart

Now in the room of borderless walls
the world is finally conceived beneath the halls

Come over the mountains my autonomous freaks
here there are no souls that can be critiqued

What are you going to do? What are you going to
do? What are you going to do? What are you going
to do? What are you going to do? What are you
going to do? What are you going to do? What are
you going to do? What are you going to do? What
are you going to do? What are you going to do?
What are you going to do? What are you going to
do? What are you going to do? What are you going
to do? What are you going to do? What are you
going to do? What are you going to do? What are
you going to do? What are you going to do? What
are you going to do? What are you going to do?
What are you going to do? What are you going to
do? What are you going to do? What are you going
to do? What are you going to do? What are you
going to do? What are you going to do? What are
you going to do? What are you going to do? What
are you going to do? What are you going to do?
What are you going to do? What are you going to
do? What are you going to do? What are you going
to do? What are you going to do? What are you
going to do? What are you going to do? What are
you going to do? What are you going to do? What
are you going to do? What are you going to do?
What are you going to do? What are you going to
do? What are you going to do? What are you going
to do? What are you going to do? What are you
going to do? What are you going to do? What are
you going to do? What are you going to do? What
are you going to do? What are you going to do?

A blast of slight deeming
utterance carved on telepathic
intermediaries
Bottleneck practice
the circus has come a long way
for the carnies to perform
Freaks
weird in misery
mire & melody
Coming together for all to
explore her charm
in ripe reward
Nostalgia is karmas
pyrrhic riddle, forever
puzzled in circled allure

What God disembarked from this exotic knot
a mild loop was remembered and the others were fair
you can run away
if you look too far
and don't see the visions
that helps us fall asleep
you can kiss her goodbye
goodbye to her all
well there are no more things we can do
so I must go
and send the ship
a letter
an answer
or a way
to feel like we're swimming amid lands
you can ease into a love
a sweet and sour
a new and old
it was repeated again
and again and again
to gain the edge
of inspected forgiveness
filled w/remorse
beginnings reminded of women
to seep the future
to claim a dinner
who will tell me
the God that made this song
for if I don't know him
she will transform me
from sin & fame

then it was medicine that cured the sick

give me a listen
give me a hand
I got words to spread
and voices to gain
as I leap in this pond
between naught & gloss
let's break our oaths
lie & affair
we can sense a season
people w/treason
monsters of Rhea
swaying along the rift
don't you know
oh, don't you go
have it be said
have me be told
wonder who masked the feathers
to float slow and soft
why were you understood
cause I need to believe
I need the odds
the gambler in me
I do this because I can
I do this when I am

Someone said we bleed in manner
harnessing the spirits of the unanswered
plucking the peaches from the branches
training the wings to fly together
                              the tempest
challenge the cliff in sullen
irresolute plunder
presenting a limp scream
in the eyes of the underfed
        deprived wildered husk
        thrown spars
cutting the buffalo
trading among grievance
                        inclined
                        denied
                        realigned
small indigenous island
native equator
steer clear from the deadly snakes

The strip-show is absorbed by a modern feel
more for us, in this deal
gather around we are about to begin
we are about to submit
our corrosive skin
the epoch of elderly was just a friend
and we watched the residents enter a crave
a measure of calculous spoon-fed inside a cave

I was turning the gears, the emblems arranged
somewhere along our raped empire
we tried to ensure our forgetful exchange
vapidly wistful in cutting the wire
the whole sky stifled, inflated, Amain
Tomorrow we sail for the merchants of Spain

And we came to America for neighbors to pray
to lay their doubts in open uncharted display
When the risk is returned to the tunnels uproar
we will peruse the sands that carry the shore
that nail the wood to the floor

Filtered by the smog of our neighboring city from
which we have continued to ignore by the presence
of an insensible sanction upon every region that
migrate to a controllable society
an indivisible monarchy
or under the proper guidance
leaves a barring question to the authority that was
incepted by a child of insufferable wealth apart
from liberation

The swamp of ten miles long
confides a preservation
insulating a helpless sky
in runt unfledged discovery
vermin nursery rhymes
conceal labyrinths residing on
wallowed invitations & lament
hollow sabals on which
callous matrimony bathes in
nourished cultivation

ghosts of the ship
maven Vikings domineering
the land before bridges
society of wanton expedition
pursuing invigorate consternation
located passed the equator
far beyond Savannah
questions capsuled in dust
paranoia legs thrilling the feet
an incredible surface of effective
apparent media w/designated
destiny

<u>Runaway Train</u>

Runaway Train
I want to stay
Runaway Train
This will end, the pain

Inside the snake alone
Where are we going, today
Our only escape, the train
No one can stop, the train
With our naked hands
The rain will never make us cold again

Is it too late for our key, to unlock the mystery
Chasing all our dreams, of our sacred plan
Endlessly in need

Passed the open gate he can't be seen or awaked
falling to a name, of his unmarked grave

A trail is found near the flooded home
Grab the rope
Deep inside the native island
Stripped from his remaining hope

Take the train, the runaway train
The only path, to escape the pain
of a somber past, evil acts in certain
ways, unsure to ever know

Take the train, all night
Take the train, & feel all right
One trip thru the end of the night

The lost girl has gone away
The lost girl has gone away
Left inside a memory

He came outside to the narrow cliffs, he looked
down on two wives searching for a lustful night
He turned around & saw the animals outside, & he
Went to the infinite prism to grab the light, then he
Took a drive along the coast, where the sand didn't
Even go, and he stepped out from the night
His legs were shaking while he began to climb up
The mountain, hot ash flew around him as he
Touched the top of the volcano, where he sat on
The ledge and felt the heat of his eternal core, he
Took the light and threw it in the Earth

Don't let me die on an unknown day
Don't let me wait for a time or place
It's my turn, when I want
On a car or train
On a drunk plane
On an accident for someone to blame
On a runaway train

Runaway train
I want to stay
Runaway train
This will end, the pain

I never got off in time
The ride took me to the other side
A separate life has been denied
Another dream has gone on by

The coast resides in the leopard's paw
fabricating the translucent rift as it carries
the injustice heat from the crooked nest
Swiftly winding the whales tune, as it circles
into the lambent wick. The crevice reclines
on drops of those who stare. Engines
conceited in the great awake of New Age Rock
Pleading to please a caller's voice
Faces momentarily evacuate the resort
and enter a trip. Merchant of exotic
monarchy how nice it is to see you again
Casus Belli among Indian burial grounds
sharing the artery w/skeletons of airport
terminals as the warrant for Normandy
stalls in pursuit of hypnotized muscles
Roaming the highway in tidal movement
a house of stairs.
Scalding the crops of corn
forging the doctor's prescription
to gesture the nuance of candid creed
you are too good for one life
but not for one death
Flying over the Mediterranean
& returning the ships to harbor
Losing jet streams of restless eve
Naming the islands one by one
and splitting the oceans into
more families of distant ping

Where the Apollo has gone
gave current amoralities a proper posture
a limit was exposed & the news went numb
the hive was amazed
we penetrated the solar axis
it could be touched w/full consciousness
nothing of this nature has been amplified
attracting us in lodestones
inveigle society enliven w/impetus in atman
studies prophesying colonial endurance
the enterprise of elapsed evil
occupies everywhere
divine dimension in a linear prospect
emerging an evidence of artifact
that coincides to a dulcified
potential of exogenesis

we cannot be a part of this curiosity need
a force of energy is felt beyond meditation
an authority imminent outside the horizon
find it and we can save time

a destination is a charter for more than hope

the natural heart of darkness

Who's going to stop us now?
Who's going to stop us now?
I need another chance
Just give me one more try
To make it all right
Waiting for my girl
I'm waiting on this world
For the day to come again
When she is out on the road
And decides to never come home
On a Sunday afternoon
Where the cars are all alone
And the people are all alone
Driving down the snow
No one's going to stop you, now
You got to keep on driving, baby
Keep on driving away
Don't turn around
There's nothing left to see
Only you can make it
If you keep on driving, baby
But our time is slowing down
Our mind is slowing down
Everything is slowing down
Everyone is slowing down
In the night we tried to run
But the evening stopped it all
We left on a Sunday afternoon

Guiltless lust parching the
limited hay
factory utopia hazed
rooms are empty
and filthy
and the danger is new
hinging the door ever so slightly
to peep right on through
can destroy a gas
& filter water
while operators dialing to
a tone
a reanimating tone

blind rats
unworn hats
Rules of manners
diseased culture
let me sing before worms
enter inside tenement vultures
I'm speaking plain today
nothing is worth work

There was a person there & he took me to a local diner, where the knives were crafted in Japanese steel. Someone came in looking for help as we sat in the bar. I went out to see a dog laying there, next to the interstate. Containing what slow vermiculation remained as the acid began to fade. I took a sheet from the imperial archive and placed it on top of her. Ancient omnipotent truth, wrapped in thick calcium. Clouds slip by & I left the pyre, jumped in a stranger's car and headed for New Orleans. Arrive at the scene of the crime, as innocent bystanders, observing from the watchtower. My mother is alive, and she is within the system. My father is away in Ushuaia, like the rest of them.

Flashing fast through the past, we bend w/time in gravity. Smooth static nights, lawful women in the tunnels of excess. I got smart and had some fun, left the kitchen in a run. Brought the rhythm to a stun, beneath the rays of the sun. Someone else is here in this room, & she was gone far too soon. Leaving nothing to do but to consume this doom that will take me to my tomb.

Under the dust of all this, concealed by the creases
of hallow trees & swept inside mounds beneath
complacent networks of narrow channels. Minerals
wiped clean w/cuts of virtuous wonder. I know this
place from a dream I had four years ago, I know this
place from the blackout. We've ripped vines from
each rooftop & attended the grand opening of
this raw feast.

It was successful, every person saw something.
Everything continued & I touched danger. Robbed
from my strenuous fight, the crossroads appeared in
moments of sure conviction. Now dawn slips into the
forge of bright lustrous silk. All was gentle, peaceful
rises in the wake of the night. Then the rattle upon
conscious bliss, sunk w/the crash
of the protected ship.

Ensure your doubts extolled so loosely
the rapid beat is gaining speed
festering a clement dilution in modus altruism
candid passage to be claimed
and a punishment is owed
                    yet to be paid
I want to greet our endeavors in the form of misery
            (desire is an adolescent of misery)
the bravery earned after each opportune existence
of the final ceremony we postponed
repurposing the Port de Singapore to become a point
of entrée

                              Currency collusion
                              Absent affusion

Did you hear, did you hear, did you hear the sheer sounds confessed? Art is dead. Art is dead, and there's nothing you can do about it. It's all ruined, the whole thing is rotten now, & from the looks of it, no one seemed to care. I want to know, I want to know who's going to save this world. What's wrong with changing the world? Why can't we do something different? Can you see it? Can you see it Seattle? Can you see it Detroit? How about you Washington DC? What about you Springfield? Are you ready to change the world, do something new? Let them know, let them know who's in charge. Let them try to tell you different. Get rid of it all, rip the walls. I want to have no rules. I want someone to set me free, I want to love the people. What are you waiting for? They want it for themselves. They want everything, & they don't even know your name. You're just a number on a scale. How does that make you feel? Is it enough to set you free? I don't know about you, but it's enough for me. Enough for us, everything must be the same. There's no room for love. Are you going to let them feed you? Are you going to be fed? Have them stir your pot? I can't eat this anymore. It all tastes the same & looks the same. Cut down from the same tree, from one giant field. Let's push them, push them till we get a new world. Till we get connection.

Who's paying for this dinner, while we stuff
the food down the fat fucking fatty's predisposed
genome sequence upon historical fuckups?
Keep the car running, I'll only be a moment.
Now wait a minute, this is all wrong. We've
been here before. A different morning &
you're still eating. Did you know, all heroes
are villains of a late arrival? Did you know,
all sounds are suspended in air? Latin is alive
& spoken by nonpolitical nomads. Old myths
of Greek rituals, immersed in mass hysteria.
My drink is so cold, I cannot feel the glass &
I'm getting out of control. Even the neighbors
put moving signs in front of their homes. No
offers have been made, as they pack their bags
& head for the nearest motel. Free rent inside
all deserted nests. The phone keeps ringing
through the night. Cars will be sold,
then furniture, followed by copper & steel.
Blindfolds of a so-called "Just System" will be
ripped off. Lady Justice, naked as the day she
was born, will not skip out on her childhood
this time. History is reintroduced by the
Indians that reside on protected native lands.
No story will go unheard. Dictators will be shot,
& all supplies of a greater life that remain
will be given away to our enterprise.

Optimal Solution
waking at the end of hibernation
conquered divinity & we raced
to the ones around us
my undisturbed curiosity will
come with me to the picket lines
for a small peek into the stained wisdom
the aftershock will come
for cities built on the edge
& a faded hunger will glimmer
with the silverware beside a resting shore

You can try to change it all
petition whatever you want to go away
build a new stadium & keep it all to yourself
grow a few things in your yard
that you so delicately care for
put on a few shirts to meet w/people
people who do the same thing
people who won't believe there's another way
but who go to movies & listen to music
eat Italian food while sitting in LA
there's more than a few in your shoes
I'd say over a billion
over a billion doing the same thing
all thinking society will reward each one of them
waiting for that day to come
not realizing they are the society
they control the reward

HEY! It's getting too darn Fast!
It's all going to the sudden Grave!
Who's trying to stop You!
Who's making these Demands!
We got to make it Last!
Till it feels all Right!
Till the music is Over!
We're going to be here for a While!
I'm looking for a good Time!
I want to feel Something!

Shivla Shikwana

Index of First Lines

30533524R00131

Made in the USA
Columbia, SC
07 November 2018